Living Under

Heaven's

Open

Windows

Gordy Carlson

ISBN 978-1-63885-259-9 (Paperback)
ISBN 978-1-63885-275-9 (Digital)

All scriptures used in this book are taken from
the English Standard Version of the Bible.

Covenant Books, Inc.
11661 Hwy 707
Murrells Inlet, SC 29576
www.covenantbooks.com

This book is dedicated to Christ followers wanting God's hand of blessing on their finances.

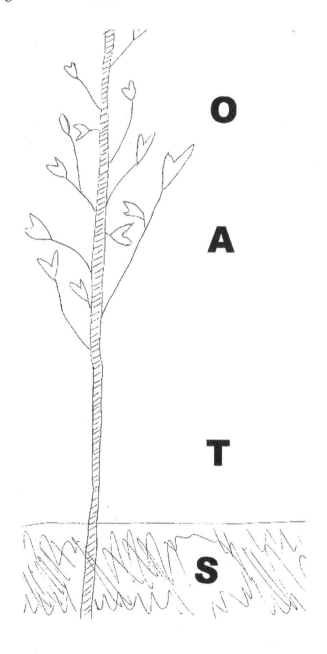

Contents

Acknowledgments

Thanks to the following:

- Jesus, for saving me, delighting in me, being patient with me, and giving me a love for writing;
- Sandra, my wife, for staying by my side as my confidant and constant encourager;
- Mom and Dad, for choosing life over death for me, even though I was not planned for;
- Dave B., my pastor for twenty-two years, who always gave me positive affirmations and opportunities to share this message;
- Rachel, my friend from the post office, using her talent for doodling to provide the drawings in this book;
- Lyman and Denise, our real estate friends, who found us our home in Anoka, the perfect place to write;
- Jane and her dog Rosie, our Mississippi River—walking friends, who always bring a smile to our faces and knowledge about this area of God's creation;
- Dan, my new next-door neighbor, who welcomed us to the neighborhood immediately, provided us both with "walking sticks," and is just a great guy;
- Joni and Chuck, Sandra's cousin and cousin-in-law, who live close by and also welcomed us into the neighborhood on day 1;
- our home church, our "storehouse" every week without fail;
- Compassion International, serving the poor with integrity for over sixty years and giving us a solid place to sow our alms; and
- Cari, Stephanie, and Hannah, incredible Christ followers who I am blessed to have as proofreaders.

Introduction

LIVING UNDER HEAVEN'S OPEN WINDOWS

It seems good to me to write this book in hopes that it will prove beneficial to many of you, the readers. Who am I to take up your valuable time? In one sense, I am a nobody, known only to family, friends, and a few associates I have met along my life's journey. Indeed, you probably would not know me from Adam. Although maybe you would. Adam would be the tall, dark, handsome, and OLDER one! I am just a common man. An uncomplicated man. One who is like most of you. Maybe that in itself will be an encouragement to you. The good news is we are all a SOMEBODY to the God of the Bible who created us. Intimately known by Him, we are all individuals with whom He can communicate. For Christ followers, this reality is what I call THE DIFFERENCE MAKER. This book came to fruition over decades of relationship building between God and me. As in any relationship, both parties must participate. I am thankful for His patience with me throughout my sixty-eight years on this earth.

Here is my background in brief. I was born in Washington, DC, in 1953. I was raised in a suburb of Minneapolis, Minnesota. When I was twenty years old, I married the only girl I was ever really serious about. She was twenty-one at the time. I like to tell people we have been married for forty-seven years—and to the same person! The only post-high school degree I have is an Associate of Practical Theology Degree from Christ for the Nations Institute in Dallas, Texas. My degree did not open up full-time employment for me. I became a blue-collar worker, working for the United States Postal Service as a rural letter carrier for twenty-nine years. My wife, Sandra, and I have three children and five grandchildren. I am now retired and working on my *bucket list*, which includes this book. This brief biography is shared with you in hopes that you will find encouragement, knowing that God can be at work in your life like He has been in mine. You are special, even if you don't feel like it, even if others don't see it. Perhaps you will someday write a book to share nuggets from your own relationship with Jesus.

I do not pretend to be a financial wizard, or to be well-versed in the workings of the stock market. This book is a simple and practical approach to money management and financial security. It has proven invaluable in keeping our financial house in order. I call it the OATS Principle. It looks like this.

Chapter 1

THE LINE

O

A

T

_____

S

I find it helpful to think of this principle as a seed to be planted in the ground. In this case, you are planting an oats seed. As you live out this principle, you might notice God reminding you of it from time to time, like when you sit down to eat your Cheerios at the breakfast table. (I personally like Honey Nut Cheerios. Sandra is the honey. I am the nut.) Perhaps the reminder will come at a time when you are weak in your faith, as an encouragement to finish the race set before you. So let's dig in.

The line between the S and the T represents ground level. A planted seed is underground, unseen to the naked eye. It cannot be seen, but it is there! Much like oxygen. We would be foolish to deny oxygen's existence. Indeed, physical death would result in any attempt to deny the existence of oxygen. Seeds grow from underground upward. Thus, the OATS seed begins unseen underground and grows upward with visible fruit. The first element of OATS is symbolized by the letter S.

Chapter 2

SERVANT

The letter S represents SERVANT. Our heart is the seed, underground, invisible to the human eye. But not to God's eye! "Man looks on the outward appearance, but the Lord looks on the heart" (1 Samuel 16:7). The true follower of Jesus has a servant attitude forming in his heart. I say *forming* because it is a lifelong process. Christ followers should desire to surrender their lives to Jesus. To be like Him. To yield to His word, the Bible. To yield to the Holy Spirit. To follow His example of coming to serve, rather than to be served. The blessings of God are given freely to those who yield their lives to follow and do His will.

Before going any further, I need to say that this book is NOT a how-to-get-rich teaching. God's blessings in my life have come in many forms. It has been rare when it has come as a big unexpected check in the mail. What I have come to notice is He has unique ways to meet my needs. It is fun to see Him at work doing this. Like a good father, He likes to surprise His kids. I think it brings Him much joy in surprising us. I think it brings Him much joy when we recognize His unexpected provision. Our God is a generous God. He is not stingy! Scripture tells us He owns the cattle on a thousand hills (Psalm 50:10). We sometimes wish He would send one of those heifers down sooner rather than later. Godliness with contentment is great gain (1 Timothy 6:6).

This is the only time the word *contentment* is found in the Bible. The position of contentment only comes through a relationship with God through His son Jesus. That is how we are deemed godly. He is worthy of our service. In serving, we discover His timing to be always perfect. We also discover there are things He cannot do. He cannot fail. He cannot lie. He cannot create a rock that is too heavy for Him to lift. He cannot be too late. He cannot abandon His children. Reaffirm your willingness to follow Him, to serve Him, even now, with a servant heart.

Chapter 3

TITHE

As our financial seed breaks ground, the first evidence of this should be represented by the letter *T*. *T* stands for TITHE. The word *tithe* means "a tenth." The concept is a simple one. The first 10 percent of our income belongs to God. Therefore, to not give back to Him what is rightfully His is robbing God. Robbing God is not a good way to have His hand of blessing on our finances.

Tithing is mentioned in the Old Testament prior to the giving of the Levitical (Mosaic) laws. Abel tithed 2,500 years before the Mosaic law (Genesis 4:4). Abraham tithed 400 years before the Mosaic law (Genesis 14:20). Jacob, 270 years prior (Genesis 28:22). Jesus's own endorsement of the tithe can be found in the New Testament in Matthew 23:23. Though Jesus's life and death fulfilled the Levitical laws and ceremonies of the Old Testament, tithing was not done away with by His resurrection and the new covenant. Other examples of pre-Mosaic laws that are still with us today are the law of gravity and the law of reaping and sowing. If you jump off the roof, you fall down, not up. If you sow corn, you get corn.

The tithing principle is described in Malachi 3:8–11:

> Will a man rob God? Yet you are robbing me. But you say, 'How have we robbed you?' In your tithes and contributions. You are cursed with a curse, for you are robbing me, the whole nation

of you. Bring the full tithe into the storehouse, that there may be food in my house. And thereby put me to the test, says the Lord of hosts, if I will not open the windows of heaven for you and pour down for you a blessing until there is no more need. I will rebuke the devourer for you, so that it will not destroy the fruits of your soil, and your vine in the field shall not fail to bear, says the Lord of hosts.

To not tithe is to rob God. To not tithe puts a financial curse on your income.

The tithe is referred to in Scripture as *first fruits* (see Proverbs 3:9–10). It is meant to be the FIRST 10 percent. The full tithe is meant for the storehouse. It is meant to be brought or given willingly. God loves a cheerful giver (2 Corinthians 9:7). Before continuing on, let me interject this fact. God will do more for you with your 90 percent left over from your paycheck than you can do with 100 percent. I have seen this up close and personal for forty-eight years. Notice God says in Malachi to put Him to the test. You will be hard pressed to find anywhere else in the Bible where God tells you to test Him. Notice also He says He will open the windows of heaven for YOU and pour down for YOU a blessing. The phrase "windows of heaven" is found in at least two other places in the Bible. When Noah entered the Ark, God opened the windows of heaven and covered the earth with rain. When Jesus was baptized by John in the River Jordan, the heavens were opened, the Holy Spirit descended, and the Father's voice spoke.

When we tithe, God saturates our lives with His provisions. When we tithe, the entire Trinity is involved in our lives; He is pleased with us. The wise person will choose to live under Heaven's open windows! Tithing is a primary indicator of your commitment to follow Jesus. I would argue it is THE primary indicator. The driving force behind this is not based on feelings. It is based on obedience and trust in God to honor His Word to you. It is for your benefit. It is a safety net for you and your family.

Tithing brings you assurance of His care and provision. Psalm 37:25 is a verse that I can shout "AMEN!" to. "I have been young, and now am old, yet I have not seen the righteous forsaken or his children begging for bread." Sandra and I have tithed from day one of our marriage. We were young. Now we are old. We still have imperfections, as do our children. But we are righteous in Christ and have never been forsaken or seen our children begging for bread. The principle is sure—you reap what you sow. Sow obedience, reap His promises.

Does God really need your 10 percent? Listen to Psalm 50:10–12. "For every beast of the forest is mine, the cattle on a thousand hills (there's those heifers again). I know all the birds of the hills, and all that moves in the field is mine. If I were hungry, I would not tell you, for the world and its fullness is mine." It is not that God NEEDS your tithe, but that YOU need to give it. Put your finances under God's hand of blessing, and you will allow no room for Satan to steal and devour what God is watching over.

The peoples of the Bible were living, for the most part, in an agricultural society. Therefore, their offerings were of the agriculture nature—crops and animals. In our society, our tithe is derived from our paychecks and other monetary transactions.

In a nutshell, I believe tithing is the FIRST 10 percent. "The best of the first fruits of your ground you shall bring into the house of the Lord your God" (Exodus 23:19). First fruits refer to GROSS income, not net income. This is easy to illustrate. If I make $10 per hour and work 100 hours, I have earned $1,000. How much did I make? $1,000. Yet my paycheck will be less than that because Uncle Sam takes out taxes. The government does not trust me to willingly give the appropriate tax to them. God, however, wants to trust me. I am on the honor system with Him. I am to honor Him with the first fruits of my produce (Proverbs 3:9).

In the above example, my tithe would be $100. I need to remember that God can do more with my $900 than I can do with $1,000.

Do we have proof of this in Scripture? Yes! God fed 5,000 men (plus women and children) with 5 loaves and 2 fish. He fed 4,000 with 7 loaves and a few small fish. He whittled Gideon's army of 32,000 to 300 before He brought a military victory. He slew big Goliath with little David. The STOREHOUSE is our home church. It is the place we go to receive our primary spiritual nourishment outside of our own personal devotion time with God. The WHOLE tithe is for our home church. Tithing is an act of worship (see Deuteronomy 26).

Worship is far more than feel-good-high-energy singing. Obedience is worship. Work is worship. A friend of mine told me this once, and it revolutionized my attitude about going to my job at the post office. We are to do everything we do as unto the Lord (1 Corinthians 10:31). Tithing is a freewill choice. Our tithe is *given* to God, not taken by God. Our tithe passes through the hands of men. That is why it is above ground and visible. Giving does not even begin until we have paid our tithe. I practice tithing on ALL MONE-TARY INCREASES whenever possible. If I have unexpected money come in, unless it is the exact amount for a current need, I tithe on it.

This follows the example of Jacob in Genesis 28:22 which reads, "And of ALL that You give me I will give a full tenth to You." We know that we can never out give God. Three of my favorite verses in all the Bible are found in Matthew 6:19–21. The key thought is verse 21. Jesus said, "For where your treasure is, there your heart will be also." I would have said it differently. I would have said, "Where your heart is, there will your treasure be also." Jesus knows our heart will follow our treasure. Can you grasp this revelation? Put your treasure in Heaven and your heart will follow. With your heart in Heaven, your salvation is secure! The devil will not steal away your soul. It is under God's heavenly care.

Tithing is meant to be a blessing, a faith builder. I KNOW God will keep me on this journey of life. He is faithful and committed to His Word. So what's in your nutshell? How is that working out for you?

Another one of my favorite verses (it is OKAY to have more than one) is Psalm 31:19. David proclaims, "Oh,  how abundant is your goodness, which you have stored up for those who fear you." When I was visiting my son Chris in Seattle, we went to the top of the famous Space Needle. From there, on a summer day, I could see snowcapped Mount Rainer. Remember, I just said it was summer. But I can see snow. That image of Mount Rainer is how I understand Psalm 31:19. It is as though God has a great big mountain of vanilla ice cream in Heaven. The ice cream represents His goodness. Every now and then, He takes His ice cream scooper and plops a scoop of ice cream out the window right into my day, no matter what season of the year it is. The ice cream doesn't melt. The ice cream refreshes my soul. The ice cream reminds me of God's heart and of His intentions for me.

God is eternal. God is good. God's intentions are eternally good. His desire, established long ago, is to pour into our life blessings. A relative once said to me, "Everything always seems to go right for you guys." I am thankful people can notice that about us. I am also thankful that people don't always see the in-between times of stress, worry, and disagreements! If you take time to read Psalm 31:19, you will notice the last eight words. God's goodness for those who fear Him is visible "in the sight of the children of mankind."

Prior to our move to Minnesota, Sandra and I spent time downsizing our home. In the new home, we realized we were short on key pieces of furniture. Over the next few weeks, God led us to new places to shop, with good-looking furniture priced down considerably that fit with our new, retired budget. Off the top of my head, I can count nine pieces of furniture that filled up our new home quite nicely. Sandra has the *gift* of finding good deals on vehicles and motorcycles. Over the years, I can recall four cars and one motorcycle at below average prices and below average mileage that she found for me in her searches. I believe it is part of the *open window* covenant God has made with us. He is not usually sending us checks in the mail, but He is leading us to a good buy when we are in need of one. It even applies to good *sells*. Our former home we listed for

$15,000, more than our realtor advised, based on what Sandra felt God wanted us to ask. To her credit, the realtor did not try to talk us out of it. To Sandra's credit, she heard correctly from God. Our home sold the day it went on the market for exactly what we were asking.

Chapter 4

ALMS

Over and above the tithe is ALMSGIVING. Though tithing is giving to the storehouse, your local church, almsgiving is specifically targeted toward helping the poor. There are numerous verses in Scripture that speak to this issue. Many of these verses have amazing promises within them. Did you know that God expects us to give to the poor? And if we do, we can expect God to fulfill His promises to us. "When you give to the needy…" Jesus said two times in Matthew chapter 6. Not IF, but WHEN. It is a financial discipline He wants each of us to establish.

Again, this is a separate discipline from the tithe. Since these are disciplines, we should practice them on a regular basis. The church will be here until He calls us home. The poor will be with us also because of sin in the world and because Jesus said so (Matthew 26:11).

There is no final payment on tithing and almsgiving. A principle is laid out in Leviticus chapters 19 and 23. This principle is called the Corners of Your Field. God's people were instructed to leave the corners of their fields unharvested, regardless of the crop. These unharvested corners were to be left for the poor and strangers. Unlike the tithe, there is no biblical percentage tied to almsgiving.

In 1985, I came upon an explanation of this principle that Sandra and I have since used in our almsgiving. It is from *The Mishnah*, a composition of various Hebrew traditions and oral laws compiled around AD 200. In *The Mishnah*, it is written that the corners of your field should be no less than one-sixtieth of the harvest. This equates to 1.67 percent. For us, we round this up to 2 percent. Thus, we earmark 2 percent of our income for the poor. If you are doing the math, this now leaves us with 88 percent to live on.

As I write this book, we have been giving alms for thirty-five years and tithes for forty-seven years. Our testimony continues to be that God will do more with our 88 percent than we can possibly do with 100 percent. I encourage you to test Him yourself. He is up for the challenge. Remember though that when you plant a seed, it takes an amount of time before you see evidence of that seed above ground. We know of two excellent churches (one is our current church), which both teach that you need to allow three months' time before you see the signs of reaping what you sow in your giving. If you persevere, you will one day thank yourself that you stuck with it for three months!

In Acts chapter 10, we read about a man named Cornelius. He was a Roman leader. The Bible describes him as a man who feared God and generously gave alms. The story of Cornelius is important to note because he is the first non-Jewish person (a.k.a. Gentile) to receive the outpouring of the Holy Spirit. There was a big window in Heaven that opened for this *almsgiver*!

As you grow in the obedience of giving, it becomes less of a test and eventually becomes a nonissue. You will simply love to give alms. Why? Because God will have proved over and over that He is taking care of you. That is our testimony. At times we have been low on finances and tempted to not give to God what is rightfully His. I resist those temptations, give what is proper, and see God sustain us until that next paycheck. His faithfulness to His Word and to His people is legendary. On a personal note, God gave me a promise in 1985 as I was considering the alms principle. I wrote these words down as they came into my heart. He said, "If you give to the poor, I will make sure you always have an income." That was a huge encouragement for me—a simple, common man, with a wife and three kids! I have always had an income. Twice, a job was created in a company for which I was then hired.

The late Billy Graham once said, "God has given us two hands, one to receive with and the other to give with. We are not cisterns made for hoarding; we are channels made for sharing." We find giving to be a great joy. I think you will too.

Where should you give your alms? This is a question you must hear from God on. There are many fine Christian organizations whose sole existence is ministering to the needs of the poor. Since 1990, we have directed our almsgiving to Compassion International, in the form of child sponsorship. It is wise to thoroughly check out your selection. Make sure the money is used primarily for ministry to the poor. Two things to look for are a high level of godly character from the top down and a track record that validates God's hand upon them. Compassion International is a ministry of high integrity whose motto is "Releasing children from poverty in Jesus' name." If you discover your alms percentage amounts to $38 per month, you are able to sponsor one child through Compassion International. And you are the only one in the world to sponsor that child. That is a very cool way to give alms! Their ministry approach is unique and brilliant. I would encourage you to check out their website. I believe we do not rightfully own our income until we have separated out the portion for God and the poor.

When you see poverty, don't feel guilty. Be grateful for what God has blessed you with, and in acts of generosity and kindness, seek to elevate others to a higher standard of living. Don't feel guilty if you are wealthy. God has blessed you so you can be a blessing to others. Throughout the Bible, the issue of the poor has always been important to the Lord. Let us, as Christ followers, be part of the solution to eradicate poverty as much as is possible.

Chapter 5

OFFERINGS

At the top of the acronym, over and above the tithe and the alms, is OFFERINGS. I make a distinction between offerings and alms. Offerings do not have to be strictly for the cause of the poor. For example, your church has established a building fund for future expansion. They are asking people to prayerfully consider making a monthly financial commitment to this fund. This would be an offering. It would not come out of your tithe or almsgiving. Other examples might be paying forward for someone in line behind you at Starbucks or at the gas station. It could be helping to meet the need of a friend or relative because you feel a prompting from the Lord. In the examples above, you may see there are two types of offerings: one is systematic (building pledge), and one is spontaneous (responding to a prompting).

I am reminded of one such prompting at a Walmart store. As Sandra and I were grocery shopping, we bumped into a dear friend, Angel (not her real name), also grocery shopping. This young woman had recently been through a divorce, leaving her to raise two young girls. In one of the food aisles, we caught up on the latest news then parted company, with Sandra and I remarking how cool it was to meet up with Angel.

Later, at a checkout line, I saw Angel also approaching the lines. I motioned for her to come in line behind us. What happened next was not planned in advance. We had her place her groceries on the counter behind ours. Angel was surprised when we included her items in with ours at check out. Afterward, we separated her items from ours in the parking lot.

This true story is not to bring any praise to Sandra or me but rather to give you an illustration of spontaneous giving. I view it as God's compassion at work. I like to define *compassion* as "come passion," passion on the move and active. We knew this act of kindness brought joy to Angel. Truth be told, the joy it brought to Sandra and me was just as real. How important it is to have our minds, eyes, ears, and hands open to opportunities God sends our way to lift up and encourage another person.

In a recent email from Angel, she recounted this story, concluding with these words, "I felt not only your love, but God's as well, through your gift…one I will never forget and one which inspires me to give in similar manners." If I want to honor God, to be a light in darkness, as He calls me to be, I must allow Him to live unhindered in me, and through me and all around me. Promptings from God become easier to recognize when we spend time in His Word. I knew at Walmart that God wanted us to do this good work. He wants our lives to be a history of good works, which He created beforehand for us to do (Ephesians 2:10). When it comes to spontaneous offerings, promptings from God need to be identified quickly, for the opportunity is now, in the present. Keep preparing yourself for this by reading the Bible. Always be open to your calling as an ambassador of Christ. Always remember, your life and finances are really His, on loan for a season.

There is a freedom and a joy in giving offerings, knowing that God is smiling down at you for your obedience and for trusting Him to meet your own needs. God is love. It is not that He has love, but that He is love! One undeniable sign of this is His generosity. Everyone can be generous to a point because everyone is made in the image of God. A Christ follower should want to be radically generous. He is then demonstrating the love of God. The nature of God lives within him. Sandra and I faithfully tithe and give alms without fail. Spontaneous offerings are in the category where, at times, we want to participate but feel unable to. Because of Romans 8:1, we have learned not to accept guilt or shame if we have a legitimate reason not to give an offering.

Perhaps you have heard the story of the three men in a church service. The offering plate was being passed around for a special offering. None of the three had anything to give. Not wanting to be embarrassed, one of them fainted. The other two carried him out! Can you give too much? Remember, earlier I said giving only begins after you have given what God commands, the tithe and alms. (Oh, how we hate that word *command*.) Can we give too much in offerings? Perhaps, but only if, in doing so, we are not providing for our own family. "If anyone does not provide for his relatives, and especially for members of his household, he has denied the faith and is worse than an unbeliever" (1 Timothy 5:8). God wants us to make eternal investments. We are His ambassadors. We are still here on a mission. We are not home yet. Do all of your giving through a prayer-filled relationship with Him, and remember to take care of those you are responsible for. He has promised to give you wisdom and peace to guide you in your sowing. Don't be reckless!

Bishop Harry Westcott of Australia made the following statement to me twenty years ago, and I have never forgotten it. "If you want to know what a person's life is all about, see where they share their money." So what is your life all about? What would others say about you? Is your life in trouble? Are your finances in trouble? Then you need God's favor—His deliverance, His provisions, His blessings. Begin to sow biblically. Remember Malachi chapter 3. God will rebuke the devourer. Ask God to watch over your finances. In our home, our money is blessed because we know it really is not our money after all. We are stewards. Let His kingdom come and His will be done, even in your finances.

Chapter 6

OBSERVATIONS AND ADDITIONAL THOUGHTS ABOUT THIS GENEROUS LIFESTYLE

There is a freedom from worry available to Christ followers in regard to money. I read the following true story that happened in 1999 in Bakersfield, California. A man bought a speedboat. On his first ride, he found it to be very sluggish. No matter what he tried, he could not  get it to perform satisfactorily. He was able to get it back to the dock where there was a marina inspection attendant on duty. The attendant gave it a thorough inspection and found everything to be okay. He then jumped into the water to inspect the underside. Immediately he resurfaced, laughing uncontrollably. Underneath, the boat was still strapped to the trailer! Perhaps you need your finances loosed from what is dragging it down. Might I suggest OATS?

Freed finances is not an endorsement for materialistic bounty. I believe Jesus has called us to *materialistic simplicity*. Lack of material wealth is not a sign of small faith. Please read Hebrews 11:37–38. Jesus said the world was not worthy of these people. Cross reference this with Luke 12:15: "Take care, and be on your guard against all covetousness, for one's life does not consist in the abundance of his possessions." Be alert to your heart succumbing to greed. Deliverance from greed is found through generosity and acts of kindness. It comes through an open hand, not a clenched fist.

The lifestyle of OATS is a disciplined lifestyle, not just when we feel like it. Feelings are like the caboose on a train. The caboose is an important part for sure, but not designed to drive the train. Have you ever wondered what God is after with your life? Consider Micah 6:8: "What does the Lord require of you but to do justice, and to love kindness, and to walk humbly with your God." Justice equals to do what is right (tithe). Love and kindness equals alms and offerings. Walk  humbly equals as a servant, humble. I believe something like the following will occur when I enter Heaven. Jesus will take me to a sea of happy faces.

"Who are these, Lord?" I will ask.

"These are the people you helped bring here through your tithes, alms, and offerings." That is my dream. I will then know that it was all worth it! Any sacrifice I gave was worth it!

While attending Christ for the Nations Institute in Dallas, Texas, I was blessed to hear Wayne Myers, a longtime missionary and friend to the school. He coined the phrase, "Live to give. Give to gain. Gain to reign." We are here on earth to give something. Otherwise, we become like the Dead Sea. Dead because it has no outlet nor inlet of flowing water. We give to gain as God opens the windows of Heaven and pours out for us blessings, blessings to give away. We gain to reign. This speaks of influence. My wife and I have been to Australia, Northern Ireland, and the Philippines. Because of God working through our "oats," we have influence throughout all the world.

Hear me on this. I am not bragging or looking for a pat on the back. We have sown into lives in dozens of countries for the sake of God's kingdom. These are places we will never physically travel to, but God is there! He is changing lives! He allows us to share in His work. He is influencing through our giving. He is a debtor to no man! We will be rewarded someday, though we feel rewarded already in joy and satisfaction. The ultimate reward will be to meet our brothers and sisters in Christ. I hope you are feeling my passion. I hope you are sensing my great desire for you to be a radical giver to the kingdom of our Lord Jesus Christ.

Radical is different from fanatical. Our culture occasionally hijacks a word from its original meaning to give it a meaning totally different. Growing up, the word *gay* had a meaning much different than what one thinks when hearing that word today. *Cool* can now mean "hot," and *hot* can mean "cool."

In like manner, the word *radical* has often replaced *fanatical* in our English usage. They are not the same! Radical means 100 percent all in, sold out, totally committed. *Fanatical* carries a degree of crazy, uncontrolled, and often destructive and unreasonable behavior.

Sports fans can be fanatical about their team (though not always destructive). Living in Wisconsin for thirty-four years provided a good illustration of this. In those years, I was a huge Green Bay Packers fan, but more than that, I was a huge Brett Favre fan (the Packers' quarterback for sixteen years). Favre was extremely beloved by everyone, or so it seemed. Sandra never became a Packers fan, but she was a Favre fan. She loved to watch him play the game. After sixteen years, he was traded to the New York Jets. His popularity continued in Wisconsin. That year, every Jets game was televised in Wisconsin. The following year, he signed with the archrival Minnesota Vikings. It was shocking for me to see how many Packers fans turned on him. All the glory years meant nothing now, as fanatical fans (not all Packers fans) spewed out mean and vicious words directed at him, verbally and on signs. Craziness took over these once radical fans. They became fanatical.

The Trinity of the Bible are radical. The Father is radical to send His one and only son to ransom us because He loves us radically (100 percent). Jesus is radical in willingly laying down His life, knowing it was the only way to cleanse us from ALL our sins. The Holy Spirit is radical. Do you realize Jesus sent the Holy Spirit to earth after His ascension to heaven? The Holy Spirit gave up His place in Heaven to live down here until we are all safely home. Radical! How about you?

Do you want to be a radical giver to God's kingdom's purposes? If you are still reading, I think you are leaning in this direction.

I read of one man whose desire was to give away 90 percent and live on 10 percent. Do you know that God does not look as much at the amount given as the percentage? Consider the story found in Mark 12:41–44. Many rich people are putting large sums of money in the offering box. A poor widow puts in two small coins. Jesus said that she put in more than all the others COMBINED. "For they all contributed out of their abundance, but she out of her poverty, has put in everything she had, all she had to live on." She was a radical giver. She caught Jesus's eye. She is forever honored in the pages of Scripture. May we all live in a way that He proudly notices us!

Percentage giving frees us from comparing ourselves to others. Notice, too, that we are not exempt from giving, no matter how poor we may be. God wants the poor to participate in giving. They need the sowing principle at work for them too. Continue to give to God and to others in greater need than you are in. Give to God from your heart. God wants to release people from poverty. Poverty was never His intention. He placed Adam and Eve in the Garden of Eden, not in the slums of Eden. Whatever else you do with your life, invest in Heaven and in people.

If you are in bondage to greed, demonstrative prayer and lightning bolts from heaven will not bring you deliverance. Giving will! From God's perspective, giving is the key to true prosperity and freedom. Giving declares our dependence on God as our only true source. The greedy sees his stockpile as his security. The generous must instead depend on the Lord as his security. This security includes lasting peace of mind from the Prince of Peace Himself.

Chapter 7

WATER THE SEED

A prayer I often ask God is, "Help me to see You, to hear Your voice, and to experience You." I see God when I am reading my Bible. It is often a struggle because my mind wanders so much of the time. I envy the disciples of Jesus. They were with him for three years. They saw so much! I don't imagine they had a problem with wandering minds! What will He do next? What will He say next? What will He ask of us? Every day there must have been anticipation walking with Jesus. Maybe it was easier for the disciples to be radical.

I find I have to revisit His Word to strengthen my resolve to be radical. I have to have my spiritual ears open to His promptings. He often talks to me (not audibly) out of the blue. Oftentimes it is on my river walk each morning. Sometimes it is in the shower! (I find it difficult to take notes in the shower. If only there were waterproof Post-it Notes!) I have to carve out times DAILY to experience God. I believe He always wants to communicate with His kids. We are not always wanting to slow down, to be still. Charles Stanley said, "Make your life one long conversation with God." In doing so, the oats plant, plus all other godly plants in our fields, are being watered. The Holy Spirit is still here. He brings the water. We SHALL reap if we faint not!

Chapter 8

Concluding Thoughts

My initial intention with this book was to make it appealing to men in particular, which meant I had to make it short! A lot of us men are not great volume readers. I don't want to lose you, men! I hope I have written enough to light a fire in you. The Bible is rich in spiritual nuggets to be mined, and not just on finances and giving. I hope you will *dig* some more. I hope you will count the cost and become radical for Jesus. Jesus is the ultimate man's man, despite what the ungodly say about Him. I hope you will know Him intimately. He is the Living Word. He is the Truth. He is worth investing your entire life in. Your generosity will result in thanksgiving to God from others. Now go have a bowl of Cheerios and give some thought to what you have just read.

Only one life, 'twill soon be past,
Only what's done for Christ will last.

—C. T. Studd

Bible promises and other verses YOU NEED to read and believe:

Genesis 1:27, 4:3–4, 7:11, 14:20, 28:22
Exodus 36:2–7
Leviticus 19:9–10, 27:30
Deuteronomy 15:7–11
Psalms 37:16, 41:1–3
Proverbs 3:9,10, 11:24–25, 13:7, 15:27, 19:17, 21:13, 22:9, 28:27
Isaiah 9:6, 58:10–11
Ezekiel 16:49
Malachi 3:6–12
Matthew 3:16, 6:3, 25:35–40
Mark 4:19, 10:21, 14:7
Luke 6:38, 11:41–42, 12:20–21, 12:32–34, 21:1–4, 22:27
John 3:16, 12:26
Acts 10
Romans 8:28
1 Corinthians 10:31, 13:3
2 Corinthians 8 and 9
Galatians 2:10, 6:7
Ephesians 2:10
Philippians 2:7
1 John 3:16–18, 4:16

Helpful material regarding the Corners of Your Field can be found at myjewishlearning.com.

A Planting Prayer

Dear Jesus, you are my sovereign Lord, the one who knows my heart.

Today I bring my finances to Your throne. I commit them into Your hands, to watch over and to bless. Please forgive me any negligence on my part in the area of the tithe, alms, and offerings. I repent and turn to You to teach me obedience in this area of my life. Please rule over my finances.

I humbly ask You to sanctify my heart, my motives, and my finances. This day will serve as a milepost in my Christian walk. It is the day my finances come under Your kingdom rule. With that understanding, I now lay my finances before You, believing Your Word to be true. Thank You for the promise of an *open Heaven* and the knowledge that if You are for me, who can be against me.

Thank You for forgiveness and for Your covenant to care for me and to meet all my needs. Thank You, Lord, for Your ever-present anointing in my life, including in the area of money.

Amen.

Name_____

Date_____

About the Author

Gordy and his wife, Sandra, reside in Anoka, Minnesota. They enjoy retirement spending time with their family, friends, and relatives; taking daily walks along the Mississippi River; riding their three-wheel motorcycle; traveling when possible; playing Scrabble; and being active in Eagle Brook Church, their home church.